The Chapbook

poems by

Charles Bane, Jr.

CURBSIDE SPLENDOR PUBLISHING

Published by Curbside Splendor Publishing, Inc., Chicago, Illinois in 2011.

First Edition

Copyright © 2011 by Charles Bane, Jr.

Library of Congress Cataloging-in-Publication Data is available upon request.

ISBN 978-0-9834228-1-5

Illustrated by Isabelle Pruneau
Designed by Karolina Faber
Manufactured in the United States of America

www.curbsidesplendor.com

"We aren't used, in this ravaged era, to poems of happiness, and yet that rarity is what Charles Bane, Jr., offers us. An offering it is, nor can we doubt that this poet conceives poetry as a sacramental endeavor, with human love as our nearest approach to the divine. He takes Buber's "I and Thou" a step further to form what he calls a "monotheism of we." Judaism is supremely the religion of reinterpretation, and this poet's embodiment of it demonstrates that historical tragedy finds its best answer in the tender bonds we form in order to choose not death but life."

- Alfred Corn,
past Guggenheim Fellow, recipient of the Levinson Prize
by Poetry Magazine, and author of nine books of poetry.

"In reading the words of Charles Bane Jr. we are given a window ~ as the windows of Saint Chapelle ~ to a rarefied art. Soft light of gradient hues, delicately sculpted and hewn just so, this is what Chagall would write if he were a poet. Each work feels as if a reflective walk. There is always the moment of slow epiphany, a soft exhalation born of knowing and living deeply. To read this book is to become a harvester of the finest in literary riches."

- Constance Stadler,
Ph D., Pushcart Prize nominee, Erbacce Finalist,
author of five books of poetry and noted literary editor.

Acknowledgements

My deepest thanks to: Gabriela Segal, Ellen Trump, Rich Follett, Connie Stadler, Diana Butler, Tim Buck, Anita Spring, Clara Macri, Priyesha Nair, Hamish Montgomery, Thierry Kauffmann, Shawn Misener, Donna Fleischer, Francesca Maese, and Alfred Corn for their constant support.

⊞ ⊞ ⊞

This book is dedicated to my father of blessed memory.

⊞ ⊞ ⊞

INTRODUCTION

On these pages, God weeps; lovers commingle, becoming one; words grow wings; fireflies glow on command; eyes become beacons to guide soul-mariners; advancing years prove the surest aphrodisiac; dead poets revivify to counsel us on the true meaning of life; the spectral veil is lifted; clouds become covers and the setting sun is a beloved's chariot. Charles Bane's Jr.'s directive is implicit: Love is all.

Judaic references are sprinkled generously throughout: the spirit of הֲלָבָּק (Kabbalah; Hebrew for 'receiving'), the esoteric set of Judaic mystical teachings intended to explore the relationship between Creator and universe, informs and uplifts every breath of these modern psalms. Love is in the air, yes; but there is wisdom as well. From "Pangea":

> We, in bed, are an early Earth;
> the Africa of me is fitted to the Americas
> of you...

Such is the work of a poet who seeks only to give – to restore an appropriate sense of awe to a jaded, weary world. Who among us can afford to decline his invitation?

- Rich Follett
Author of *Silence, Inhabited: Poetic Reflections on Surviving Childhood Sexual Abuse,* and *Responsorials (with Constance Stadler).*

Table of Contents

The Two

I think when God
walked shy to Moses,
stars clustered in his hands,
he led our rabbi down
to the orchards of the heart.
The two walked near the other
and traded dreams like brothers
before sleep. They paused
afield and watched the sun,
lifted by themselves in unison,
race overhead. And Moses knew
not to disappoint this man
with faltering steps or speech.
God wept uncomprehending
of his artistry and Moses scratched
some lines in stone to honor
a beloved friend.

Picasso's Guitar

❋❋❋

is disassembled and rebuilt
on canvas when figs are sugared
and clustered in the heavens and the studio
is silent; he makes short work of it,
and in the morning gives it only a passing
glance as it lays under a window and a dovecot.
He reaches instead to paint horses yellow and blue
that are streaming up a hillside like smoke, and when he
stops to look past the guitar and through the window
the fruit and birds are one.

❋❋❋

I Wander the Beach Sometimes

I wander the beach sometimes where men stand with pants rolled,
fishing for shark. And I think I can find you in the wandering night
and set you close and kiss and, as we close our eyes,
make another universe in our private dark. And the sheets
will be like the linens dry upon the air and folded in the light when the
hurricane has gone away. You make words as I do. Make them into wings as I
will and meet me now.

Let me give you strength, again and again as night does; let me
enter into your secret and make it mine. Let me pace to you
again and over and set a step to upper door. We will fly inside. There,
the fishermen cast golden nets and you are a child again and I and you
are mine. Take this: it spills and sings, and looks for night. I rest
until light stirs, and wakes more words. Words, towns of words. A nation
of words to conquer my prize.

For you, colored flowers that sleep and dream beneath the snow
are waked and given drink and asked to form in circle about your loving
face. I borrow an hour of summer light to keep them new, and rich
as the windows of Sainte Chapelle; a jeweled room in France
catches music from stars and pipes it like the flowers. Fireflies lie
as diamonds on the frozen ground. A torch of them are not like you,
but stir when you are pleased. For that alone, they're melted.

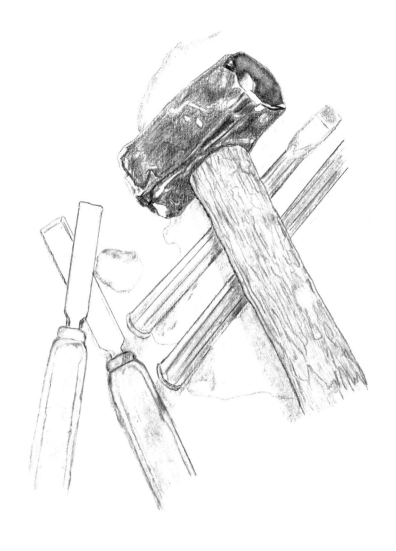

Come Si Dice

◉◉◉

Michelangelo cannot catch his breath. He
says nothing to his companions. How do you
say, the dust is numberless lights that fall
in fiery trails on clothes and hair and moving
hands? How do you say I labor here as the Maker
made, in shrift, a whole that echoes in my
every strike, and bathes my face
in rain? My hands move
in dreams I cannot show. Go home,
take wine. My neck lies on David's like a brother.

◉◉◉

We, in bed, are an early Earth;
the Africa of me is fitted to the Americas
of you. Your hair flows unerring
through the crook of my arm and the river of it parts,
as was meant,
at my fingers. Nutmeg wafts not across a dividing sea,
but fresh from lips to waiting mouth. Just below your eyebrows,
two lights guide my mariner soul, that aglow, travels
back to your same sky. We match only we, and your
face will not look distantly for mine nor lose my hand's
geography.

We Trooped Into Countryside

◎◎◎

We trooped into countryside,
walking behind tanks like children
trailing parents to a scene of petty
wrong. I was more exhausted
than I can say; I was tired of shots
and the substitute of guns for
the soundings of the sky and handsome
forks of gold like those back home
where storms are welcome to the eye.
This was a naked place, powdered
everywhere with dust and ash. It lay
on trees and covered men I shot
like birds and who dropped a little
distance away. At home,
the cathedral of the night
catches in its hands
our talk sometimes and you hear
the flight of the unseen
to firesides they crave.

◎◎◎

I like when we are in bed and I kneel
behind you and look out the window
at your dress gold and stretched
on ocean waves. I like being your shell
as you press underwater to a beach
to lay your eggs in buried sand.
I watch your lovingness, sweeping
sheets in an ancient rite appearing
from the sea. My darling, I break
on thee.

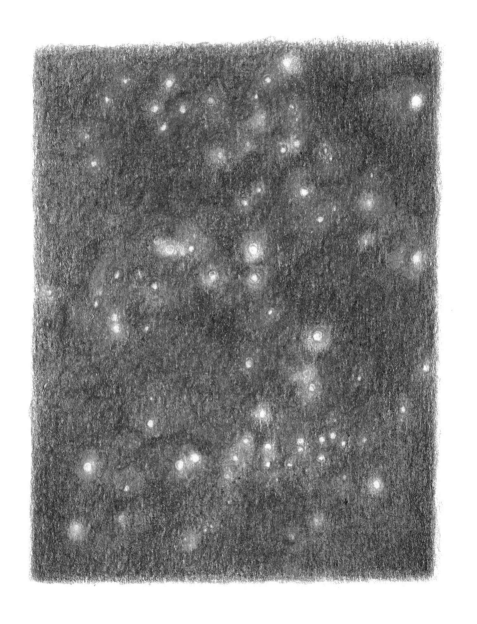

❀ ❀ ❀

Alexander's Seizure

□ □ □

It is an aloneness, this malady.
It hurled me from Bucephalus yesterday.
I fell (as I lay and shook
upon the fields) into the sea. There are always
dolphins waiting; in beautiful depths
I take a fin and watch patterns cross
the bodies of my companions that are cut from cloaks
of waves, or handsome shields. I wish the world
was watery. Swords are only flashing schools,
motioning past. The dolphins turned
to shallows and I cried, but made only bubbles.
I could not call, "Away from war. I watched you swim
at twilight once, and looked on peace."

□ □ □

Shakespeare Writes His Wife

I roamed today and saw the
sovereign. Sweet wife, she is such as we; do
you remember our long walk, when the banns
were published, and a lark was startled into flight?
She is such, save this: there is but one of her on wing.
Her train wound past; a mother with a newborn
rushed to her carriage. On the instant,
swords were drawn. The lighted bird
stopped them with a finger.
Good wife, the mother held an infant formed
to bask in higher fields. Gloriana leaned
and, both hands on the toddler's head,
whispered to the parent. Gallants
stared at what a country man
knew at once. Here was a chick being given drink.
Sweet, is she not as we, when you nest alone
and I lay below an eave?

Isn't It Amusing?

Isn't it amusing that they think
we're too old for... and don't see
when our passion stirs?
They don't notice your hand
reaching over to arrange my letters
in the middle of the game.
Do you know I love those hands
most tenderly when they're making
tea? And then, again, in the middle
of the night when you touch my arm
and, wordless, ask me to begin a ballet.
You know, I think making love to you
starts in the music of steps in snow
or your look into your purse for a lozenge
when my mouth is dry. Yes, that's the flag,
that's the pointing daystar.

Fire touches fire and in
the meeting is put out
til morning when we, in bed,
watch it rising from the east.
Such are we and all,
Other, from the ticking of
the first star. And all about
is rounded and curved that
we might find a pathway home.
All is made for but a little time
of light, and the light itself fashioned
by love for blazing kind. Here is
the truth, Other, that I read in my
twin's eyes: this space is all,
this patch for us between dark
and innocent dark. This waiting bed,
these sheets, this torch I hold. Fire
comes to fire, and mimics first light.

Untitled

I dreamt I lay beside your rose
and touched a chord that brought a whisper
from your lips. I dreamt I slipped
inside and felt a firmament and motioned now
with you, ablaze. I dreamt of petals
holding me in the magic of the dark,
and the incense of a flower.

A Father's Pen

❖ ❖ ❖

I weep as I write my
remembrance of the hour
when I and my now-lifeless
son played inside the panes
of an imperishable vacuum.
Upwards we climbed
the sheer towers of its scope
and beholding in wonderment
its vantaged range, stood
enfranchised citizens
of a creation everlasting,
unfolded in the vista of a sleeping
star. Thence, down we walked
the old and rusted ways
of a pencilled landscape,
above whose trails
a garden fared,
chaired in a traffic
of its own engendering seed.
My dearest precious one.
My priceless, sweetening bloom.
Such was the separation of myself
from my soul's light
that, seeing his features through
an imaginary lens

words chosen for my
work would stay near
a moment longer;
but of those rows
and the vocabulary of their weighing
stones, is the labor of my canto.
I pray that in its meter's
brief life upon the page
each note will plunge
upon its spot as rain
upon the feeding deep,
and plumb the sense
of fellow men.
Surveying their topography,
I rode to town on business
once, and, in a coffee house
at travel's end, turned to see
in a smoky recess shunned by other
patrons, two old sodomites.
One face had a slant, as when
a falling shower makes circles
of the dark. Both had a dignity
of their own design,
but so frail was its preserve
that a clumsy step would be
accompanied by a shatter.
Their display was bare
of an overhanging span,
but for the roof they found
below my ruby petal.

❖ ❖ ❖

Blackfoot Camp, Two Medicine Territory, (1870)

You must go from here. This is not good.
There was a raid today. Many times I counted coup.
But where I should have seen an enemy, I saw you
and my face was soft. You must go away. But then
I would follow I think to fold grasses for your sleep. I see
you gone and I cannot breathe, it stops inside
like winter. It is not my way. Why are you more than the space
that makes me ache? You have the favor, I think,
of the wavering sounds and light at end of day,
and of ancestors who linger at its edge to hear our whoops
before they wave. I cannot think of horses or plans or
blood. You warm my hands in dreams of fire. You delight
me as the bird that stops the silence of the night. I go,
to walk and seek the counsel of water.

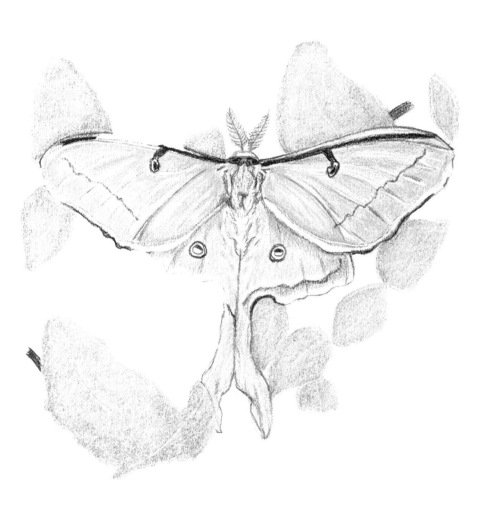

Because the heart is a climbing hill
and you are near its' rise. Because
you are near when far, and I feel ever
close; because bells are not only for towers
but I too as your name knows.
Because forever is a length of string and
neither lets go. Because the secret self
can be given free, and after, glows inside,
whole.

Robert Frost

☐
☐
☐

What does it mean, in the end? Am I the wood
I dreamed, a handsomeness of gold and shadow
girls reach to with a hand? No, I am a moment
at a Chautauqua when inhabitants gather round
a bandshell. For a moment I am aired
by a girl or boy of creamy face and made alive
in a nervous pace. The men listen for a hint of something
true, wives raise a finger to lips and children at once
are quiet and finish their ice cream. I say that their town
will disappear at night into the surrounding prairie
like a star from a highboard into a swimming pool below
and the arch and upraised arms and legs pressed just so
is an act of gracefulness, or bowl they should sup from
as it stands plain on table and catches summer sweat.
The recitation's done; my ashes are scattered over
the fairgrounds, and my white hair drifts overhead
and away from there.

☐
☐
☐

Homeless Vet on Congress Avenue

◈

I can see that when traffic at your corner's stopped,
and flashing lights in blue and red signal the arrival of our escort,
you will be disconcerted; soon, an altar boy will be beside you
and staring down at his calm face, you will calm in turn.
We must arrive at the basilica at the perfect light of day,
the perfect honored hour. Of all waiting inside, not one
does not feel a hollow and a fear that he or she will fail.
They bend in arcs of grace as doors open to ceremony
and looks from a country foreign to your every day
flood the interior. This is gallantry of forgotten kind to you, beloved
of me, who slept in viaduct and were rolled by boys who made
you curse. Rain halted fitful sleep. Coins of light showering
down make known what is put away. Music rains on nave and aisle
as even on the sunniest day. Does it not halt
your walk with speech that gives more than we,
all those times we sped as you stood bare? Does it
not make a hundred baths for a thousand lonely days? Step and
step forward once again, for if you wake then I too, I swear, will slay
the light that lies. You must reach the apse. You must reflect windows
more bejewelled than these, if we are not to perish in the dark and refire
in your mercy. We await you at the front, we teem beside columns and
pictured scenes of sacrifice pale and unworthy of modern pain. Step and
step again with boys long practiced in procession. Forgiveness is the only
faith worth wearing as a vestment. Reach the dome, turn and say, Dona
Nobis Pacem.

◈

◈

It is Night; Shall We Be Together?

It is night: shall we be together?
Shall we move into the flame
that reaches from your table
to a sky without a breath of God
but for what we make in genesis
when sleep is swept away? Shall
we set birds and gentle deer upon
the field where I am utterly undone?
My love, I did not know you
could bring light so close I
would hunger at my work
for dark.

Harry Truman as a Child

◻ ◈ ◻

The fields were boxed into sounds, weren't they,
as carefully as books beside your bed, and a
necktie draped for the next day on a chair? And
you owned it all, didn't you? You owned the
priceless fields and start of day as warm as
Mama's voice. You owned the inexpressible,
the catch in the throat, the joy that was not
stopped because it was not seen. And
then Mama bought you glasses, and you were
confirmed as prince of strawberries and the only
boy in the county with spectacles. I understand,
Harry. It was Mama who saw you listening to the
fireworks instead of watching, and took you to
the doctor. Your mother, my father. The days
blaze, don't they? Aren't they amazing, those
lilting sounds? Every biscuit,
every goat? Every single
passing train? The fields like
linen that can't be soiled?

◻ ◈ ◻

There Is No Safety

There is no safety
beyond these walls;
but here you are
enclosed in all of me
and all I waited for
before the grace of you
appeared. I know
the length of winter
snow on lighted panes
like stretching arms that
turn to fragments in the
cold. I watched them
fail and promised myself
that you would come,
and find me whole.

I dreamt of you together
in a sunny field, walking
to me, smiling. Is this true? Do
you pass from hand to hand what
here falls in common light? Is this
within your power? Mother, do you
kiss the necks of bathing souls and laugh
when you lower your Brownie? Are there
trains and trips to the city, and Mother,
is there refinement befitting such as you?
Did you find Ollie? Weep and brush his shoulder,
and tell him when he was downed you were crushed
like paper?
Tell me you are there. Tell me you keep heaven coins
Dad would lose and spot clouds parting the horizon. Tell
me my beloveds, does innocence crowd you round
as we did all? Part, Mother, as boys did in Forest Hills
when you walked, smiling, to the subway entrance,
unbelieving you lived near?
Beloveds, we are well: life is Spring unsoiled in those
of us you carried.

In the Fall, oak leaves blew as we
in the courtyard of the Art Institute. It
was afternoon now, and my brother drew in
charcoal. In the morning we had flittered in
the galleries, and lighted on a Van Gogh, and
pecked Vincent's chairs of straw. We whisked away;
we were afraid of Vincent's fields, and broad strips
of hammered spell. We fell into a Chagall and I saw
my brother bow his head in a reverence of night. Then,
out again. I followed my brother, I did as he. I bent
in wheat and held a scythe, or watching him, made
merry like a star. I reached as he, eyes shut,
to grace. Now I sat in the falling day and watched
him sketch, the leaves identical as we.

In a little room
like this, long ago,
phantoms were slain
in the dark. I stared
into an abyss and after
I was less afraid. I want
ever to be unchanged;
shall we lay and dare
the rain falling in shadows
on the walls? Shall we say
that we will dip into the deepest
place and with handfuls
of unquenchable strength,
ease the worried small? As they
sleep, shall we fit the young
in armor of the brave?

Poem For My Son

It must be carried in the hands, this such as never was. Allowed
in shadow, a second of nevermore? Out from the shadows this precious,
darling, lamp. Onto throne of day, this unhoped for. This song,
and miracle of dancing light. This reach of waiting mine.
A leap into my arms; birds watching, winging life atop the house where we
race to spill upon the floor and map its' world in play. Sending
clouds like ships to farther skies in the park at close of day. Night
falling like arms upon the sea. Sleep, love atop love. Sleep,
and turning in the bed, change dark to eyes of God.

Cycle

The sun is cracked and spills itself,
and stains the border of the western sky;
and we must find a bed where I may pour in you
a sea of stars from which light comes,
unshadowing the hillsides of your near
form and spreading,
becomes the original poem.

The Sabbath Bride

I am at synagogue tonight
and when we turn to face
the Sabbath Bride, I am walking
with your elbow in my palm to the corner
restaurant. A boy came past and cursing,
muttered, "Dirty Jew." I wheeled and punched
and he fell to the sidewalk. He had a bloody
mouth. I leaned over him and yelled -like he was deaf -
"Do you know me?" He nodded. I yelled
again, "You know I live there, at 369
Walnut Street?" Again, he nodded. I bent
down. "And you are Krzysztof, the baker's son,"
I said, and saw his eyes widen, "And if you tell
your father or friends about this, I'll do it again.
Understand?" I turned, and ushered you
into the restaurant and to a table.
I felt ashamed then. You looked at me
and said, "There's blood on your shirt."
I looked down. You excused yourself and left.

I was so angry with myself. I said aloud,
"Why did you behave like that,
and scare off that pretty girl?" You
returned from the restroom with napkins
wetted in the sink. You looked at my eyes
and said, " Lean forward". I knew we'd
be husband and wife. I never dreamed
we'd be married so long. I didn't know
love could be so easily carried, or for
such a distance. I blink,
and return to synagogue. We turn
and face the sanctuary door. Dearest,
I am waiting.

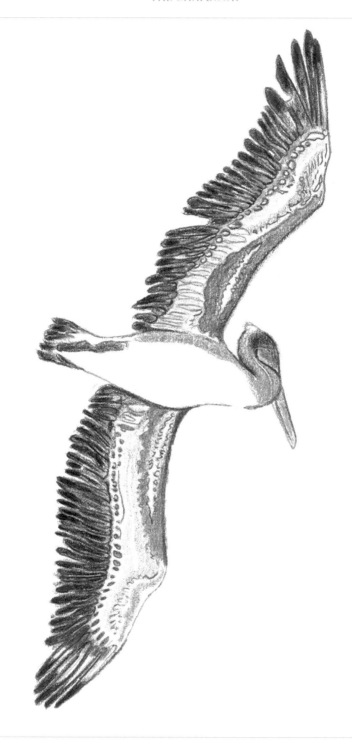

I Must Write

I must write to you; no,
that is not right. I must
take you to myself, a child
who speaks of pleasures
you have never known:
looking through a sextant
and seeing at my feet a length
of rope, coiling like the sun. Shall
I say we were once becalmed
until the wind fell upon our sails
like your lovely hands and we
struck for home? Is it
possible that in the garden you
could not feel the passing of yourself
like a Creator before
the only man to view
that loving face? It is a wonder
to a mariner that longitudes
can be erased and the bounty
of the earth heaped inside
my arms. My dearest, I must
embark; I send this on
other feet. I will pace
upon the roiling sea and think
that islands rising in the dawn
and winging friends from shore
are signals of your lift of me
from dust to follow
in your wake.

Countless Nights

Countless nights I've covered you
in clouds and slept nearby. I dream
you are stoking stars within
and forming constellations of a universe
that rushes to my arms. I dream
history's unchained and you and I
are as when I found you, an island
at my center. Change to worlds
of light, and tender dreams.

Then We Came Home

Then we came home;
your fingers pushed my hair,
grew flowers in the ash
and I was young.
I loved you and wrote
of it in candlelight. Je t'aime,
I wrote. You stirred
and I returned to bed. Then,
we made ourselves a single,
breathing soul.
Stars made fireworks,
the sea travelled
in a coat of sparks
and we stopped
the hours.

I came upon you
when I was a child
and kept the memory
close, through every
feverish year. My hair
was silk from corn; yours,
black as the birds upon the snow
I fed the winter long. I opened books
at night and looked at barest
trees and wished for Spring. I watched
for leaves birthing like the stars. I made
poems, and saved the lights I found
waiting in my marrow. One day I would tell
you of the music I heard between its honey-
combs and followed til words rested
on a page. You would understand. You
would hold the glass and pour my amber
work until it filled you to a brim.
You would say, this flames the trees
and you are the harvester of my soul.

My old soul has sung before.
It has lain many hands in mine;
I reach for yours, and link it to he
who needs. He stands in Bergen-
Belsen in the rain, waiting his turn
to expire. He takes hands he cannot
save and sighs and breathes
the gas. He is a petal;
I see inside his heart. I love you as
he and they who follow down
the stairs. My hand takes yours and hers
and his. Be careful of their souls, they
are little suns. They rise in me and flame
the sanctuary where we stand, betrothed.

When Something Closes In

When something closes in
that changes or seems
to change the prospects
of the day, I think of you
and your voice on the phone.
I hear waves of you returned
from space in sound that circles
half in dark, half in light to find
my waiting call. Baby, you say
and I take my cell outside and
standing, lift my face.

Untitled #2

A cloth of rain
hangs before a
single, yellow lamp
and seated in a
cafe I stare into
your eyes that
search in sleep
for me. An older
patron starts at
the thunder and
remembers arms
upraised by men
in endless rows who
long ago waited
patiently to be shot
and remembered
home only as a
dream. My love,
we are fevered and
washed by every hope
that splashes here
on folded leaves.

In the Hotel

In the hotel, unlocking
doors of time and space,
I knew we were met when
each was newly made. I knew
the laws were dust like dying
stars and worshipers lifting scrolls,
jeweled and dressed, are blind.
My love, I follow until the expiration
of the sun; my grail lays sleeping
far away and turns her head
alone; but an arc of burning dreams
hurries hours away and lashes
the horses of our wait.

Come Beloved

◎ ☀ ◎

I am hungry; come soon. I looked
tonight at flames like you upon
the west and jewels winging
home. I hold you in my eyes
when I see what cannot
be stamped again. All the earth
is of a kind but for the rarities
that clamber unknowing of their
gifts on vales of purest light,
and look at the common life
of us in shade. Come beloved,
soon.

◎ ☀ ◎

About the Author

Charles Bane Jr.

is a native Chicagoan and a globally published poet. His work has appeared in print and online at The Indian Diary, The Criterion: An International Journal in English, Clutching at Straws, Durable Goods, Word Pond, and museumviews.com. His poetry was included in *I Was Indian: An Anthology of Native Literature, Vol 1* (Foothills Publishing). He was the only non-Native American included in the volume. In addition, his writing has been the focus of critical review, most recently in *The Poetry of Charles Bane, Jr.* in The Calliope Nerve. This is his first chapbook.

Certain poems in this book have been previously published as follows:

"Picasso's Guitar", and "Mother and Father"
appeared at museumviews.com.

"Homeless Vet on Congress Avenue"
appeared at Praxilla.

"Poem For My Brother", "Diana Butler", and "Alexander's Seizure"
appeared at The Calliope Nerve.

"We Trooped Into Countryside"
appeared at Clutching at Straws.

"Come Si Dice"
appeared at Wordpress.

"You"
appeared at Back Room Live.

"Robert Frost", "Blackfoot Camp", "Two Medicine Territory",
and "Untitled"
appeared at The Indian Diary.

"My Old Soul" and "Untitled 2"
appeared at Word Pond.

"Come Beloved"
appeared at Curbside Splendor.

About the Illustrator

Isabelle Pruneau

photo: Rémi Guertin

was born and lives in Québec City. She studied Art History in Montréal, obtained a Master degree in Visual Arts, Université Laval, Québec. Her work has appeared at the single-woman exhibit at Les Ateliers du Roulement à Billes, group exhibits at La Galerie des Arts Visuels, L'Oeil de Poisson, Pavillon Alphonse Desjardins. She is an associated member of the engraving workshop Engramme.

About the Type and Design

The poems in this book are set in **Perpetua**.

Perpetua is a typeface that was designed by English sculptor, typeface designer, stonecutter, and printmaker Eric Gill (1882–1940).

Though not designed in the historical period of transitional type, Perpetua can be classified with transitional typefaces because of characteristics such as high stroke contrast and bracketed serifs. Along with these characteristics, Perpetua bears the distinct personality of Eric Gill's letterforms.

Eric Gill first became famous for the typefaces he designed: Perpetua (1929-30), Gill Sans (1927-30), and Joanna (1930-31). Eric Gill attended art college in Chichester before studying under Edward Johnston at the Central School of Arts and Crafts in London.

Between 1913 and 1918 Eric Gill produced fourteen reliefs with scenes for the Stations of the Cross for Westminster Cathedral in London. In 1918 Eric Gill co-founded the Guild of St Joseph and St Dominic, a religious community of craftsmen. In 1920 Eric Gill co-founded the Society of Wood Engravers.

Eric Gill designed book layouts and most of his typeface designs date from around 1930. From 1928 Eric Gill had his own printing press at Speen, Buckinghamshire. He received commissions from bibliophile publishers, including Golden Cockerel Press, Cranach-Presse in Weimar, Leipzig publishers Faber & Faber, J.M. Dent & Sons, and the Limited Editions Club (established in 1929).

Eric Gill executed numerous book illustrations, woodcuts, graphics, and watercolors, which are mainly devotional in content.

Source: Wikipedia.com (2011).

Book design and layout by Karolina Koko Faber   karolinafaber.com